What's on the Truck?

Marvin Buckley

Trucks help us to move things.
Trucks carry things from place to place.

truck

2

Workers load things onto a truck.

Trucks go from fields to factories.
What's on the truck?

strawberries

factory

Strawberries are on the truck.
Farmers grow strawberries in fields.
Trucks take the strawberries to a factory.
The strawberries are made into jelly at
the factory.

Trucks go from factories to stores.
What's on the truck?

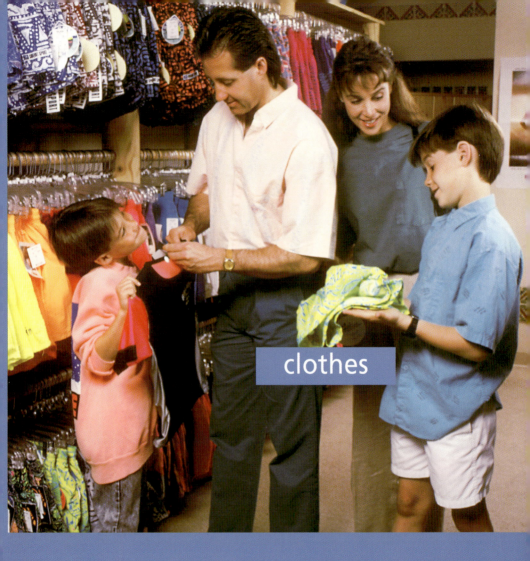

clothes

Clothes are on the truck.
Clothes are made in factories.
Trucks take the clothes to stores.
People buy clothes in the stores.

Trucks go from stores to homes.
What's on the truck?

refrigerator

home

Refrigerators are on the truck.
People buy refrigerators in stores.
Trucks deliver them to people's homes.

Trucks go from homes to other homes.
What's on the truck?

Our furniture is on the truck.

We are moving to a new house.